Farmyard at the Fair

by Holly Harper

illustrated by Beth Hughes

Wow! The fair is in town.
Fair
Can we go this year?

We need to finish on the farm. Then we might go tonight.

Dad shears the sheep.

Moira and Kear sort the wool.

Dad coils the cord.

They pack up the gear.

Look! The animals are off to the fair.
Fair

Toss the quoit on the target!
Can I join in now?

Can you hook a pair of ducks?
quack

Dad looks for the animals.

Moira looks at the sheep.

Kear hears a moo.

The cow might be near.

Ow! My beard! Shoo!

They look near the red chair.

The chicken is in the air.

They coax her down with corn.

They go back to the farm.

The animals had fun.

Now Moira and Kear can go.

Look Back

Encourage students to use the pictures to retell the story.